A cat in a pot

Speed Sounds

Ask your child to say the sounds (not the letter names) clearly and quickly, in and out of order. Make sure he or she does not add 'uh' to the end of the sounds, e.g. 'f' not 'fuh'.

Consonants

Each box contains one sound. Focus sounds for this story are circled.

f	l	m	n	r	s	v	z	sh	(th)	ng
										nk

b	c	d	g	h	j	p	qu	t	w	x	y	ch
	k											

Vowels

Ask your child to say the sounds in and out of order.

a	e	i	o	u

Ditty 1 A cat in a pot

Story Green Words

For each word ask your child to read the separate sounds, e.g. 'b-u-s', 'p-oo-l' and then blend sounds together to make the word, e.g. 'bus', 'pool'. Sometimes one sound is represented by more than one letter, e.g. 'th', 'oo'. These are underlined.

cat	hot	sun	dog
ran	hid	pot	

Red Words

Red words don't sound like they look. Ask your child to read the words but if he or she gets stuck read the word to your child.

<u>th</u>e   no

A cat in a pot

Do not read the ditty to your child first. Point to the words as your child reads. If your child gets stuck on a word help him or her say the sounds and blend them together.

Re-read the words to your child to help him or her remember what he or she has read. Discuss what is happening on each page.

a cat sat in the hot sun

but then a dog ran up

the cat hid in a pot

no cat

Ditty 2 On top

Story Green Words

For each word ask your child to read the separate sounds, e.g. 'b-u-s', 'p-oo-l' and then blend sounds together to make the word, e.g. 'bus', 'pool'. Sometimes one sound is represented by more than one letter, e.g. 'th', 'oo'. These are underlined.

fox   top   cat

hen   bug

Ask your child to read the root first and then the whole word with the suffix.

get → gets

Red Words

Red words don't sound like they look. Ask your child to read the words but if he or she gets stuck read the word to your child.

of   <u>th</u>e

On top

Do not read the ditty to your child first. Point to the words as your child reads. If your child gets stuck on a word help him or her say the sounds and blend them together.

Re-read the words to your child to help him or her remember what he or she has read. Discuss what is happening on each page.

the fox gets on top of the dog

the cat gets on
top of the fox

the hen gets on top
of the cat

the bug gets on top

of the hen

Ditty 3 A wet cat

Story Green Words

For each word ask your child to read the separate sounds, e.g. 'b-u-s', 'p-oo-l' and then blend sounds together to make the word, e.g. 'bus', 'pool'. Sometimes one sound is represented by more than one letter, e.g. 'th', 'oo'. These are underlined.

bed   mat   ba<u>th</u>   wet

Red Words

Red words don't sound like they look. Ask your child to read the words but if he or she gets stuck read the word to your child.

<u>the</u>

A wet cat

on the bed

on the mat

in the bath

a wet cat

Questions to talk about

Read the questions aloud to your child and ask him or her to find the answers on the relevant pages. Do not ask your child to read the questions – the words are harder than he or she can read at the moment.

Ditty 1

What is the cat doing at the start of the story?

What does the cat do when the dog runs up?

Why did the cat hide in the pot?

Ditty 2

Which animal gets on top of the dog?

What goes wrong when the bug gets on top of the hen?

What sort of things can fit on top of one another?

Ditty 3

Where is the first place that the cat chases the mouse?

How does the cat get wet?

How did the mouse get into the bath?

Speedy Green Words

Ask your child to read the words clearly and quickly — across the rows,
down the columns, and in and out of order.

sat	a	in	dog
on	cat	sat	cat